FREE VERSE PRESS
a Free Verse, LLC experience

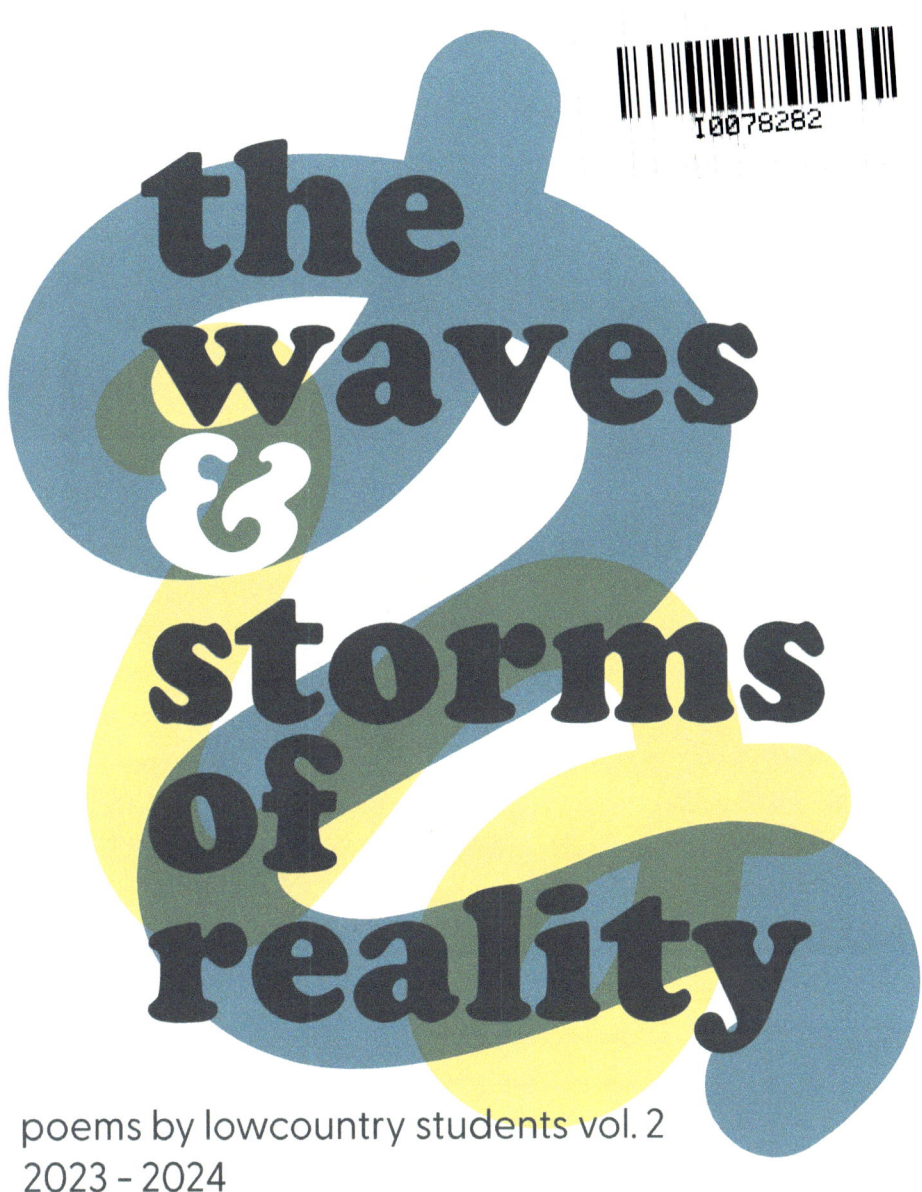

the waves & storms of reality

poems by lowcountry students vol. 2
2023 - 2024

Copyright © 2024 Free Verse, LLC

The boring, but important stuff. Does anyone actually read this? All rights reserved. No part of this publication may be reproduced, distributed, or transmitted in any form or by any means, including photocopying, recording, or other electronic or mechanical methods, without the prior written permission of the publisher, except in the case of brief quotations embodied in critical reviews and certain other noncommercial uses permitted by copyright law.

For permission requests, write to the publisher, addressed "Attention: Permissions Coordinator," at freeversepublishing@gmail.com

ISBN: 979-8-9871632-1-4

Book design by Marcus Amaker

Printed in the United States of America.

First printing edition 2022

Published by Free Verse Press
Free Verse, LLC
Charleston, South Carolina

table of contents

8. Academic Magnet High School
10. Cane Bay High School
12. Charleston County School of the Arts
16. Goose Creek High School
66. Laing Middle School
68. Moultrie Middle School
84. Porter-Gaud School

dear readers,

Being published is an experience that should be available to all writers ~ especially those in classrooms.

That's why I asked for teachers and scholars to send poems. Raw poems. Weird poems. Funny poems. Heartbreaking poems.

I want to ensure that the authentic voices of students have a chance to be absorbed, because I still hear a false narrative that 'kids' brains are going to be ruined because of AI' or 'kids are always on their phones.'"

Well, I'm here to remind you of the depth that is being overlooked.

Our young poets have embraced the spirit of freedom and self-expression. Thank you, readers, for honoring that energy.

If something makes you uncomfortable, keep reading. If something makes you laugh, keep reading. Just keep reading ...

— Marcus Amaker

Charleston, SC's first Poet Laureate
South Carollina Literary Hall of Fame
Charleston Gaillard Center Artist-in-Residence Emeritus
Academy of American Poets Fellow

Academic Magnet High School

The Man and the Sun

There was once a man who waltzed with the Sun every night. The constellations would play cellos and violins, the galaxies would sing. The Sun was bright and shimmering, with hair as long as the universe and eyes marbled and shining like the milky way. The man had always looked up to the Sun, staring till his eyes burned and light spotted his vision. He spent every day in the Sunlight, afraid of the dark that would chase away Light, and sobbed when clouds blocked the Sun. One night as he lay, falling asleep, the Sun streaked down from the sky, lighting the night, down to the ground, and paused beside his window and melted the glass. She took his hands, filled him with the needed Light, pulled him up through the clouds, through the frigid misty air, but he wasn't cold. She showed him her starry, airless home, and how the gases that She was made of helped her stay alive for millenia. The small bits of oxygen She did not need She gave to the man. The man and the Sun danced around the planets, night after night, or perhaps it was day, for the Sun always shone, and they fell deeply in love. He would always be burnt, hair singed and red welts across his face, but he loved the Sun so much that he did not notice, or maybe he just did not care. His skin bubbled and boiled, enduring painful reds and yellows. His eyes began to blur, and the Sun was only a blazing spot in his sight. He tried to tell the Sun that he couldn't see but She wouldn't listen, She did not notice, or maybe She just did not care. As the man shrank, frying to a crisp, he wanted to leave but the Sun was the only warmth in his life, Earth was so cold and so dark compared to her hot, luminous light. He stayed till his end, the last bit of him blurring away, dissolving to space, becoming stardust, sucked by gravity into the Sun.

- Elena B.

Cane Bay High School

I'm Sorry

"I'm Sorry," words I know all too well.
"I'm Sorry," the words I muttered when I fell.
"I'm Sorry," for calling myself fat.
"I'm Sorry," that I wore this hat.

"I'm Sorry," for when I feel depressed.
"I'm Sorry," for when I feel underdressed.
"I'm Sorry," I say these words every day.
"I'm Sorry," I will say these words anyway.

"I'm Sorry," that I hold in how I'm feeling.
"I'm Sorry," the world has shattered my thinking.
"I'm Sorry," when tomorrow I'll feel the same.
"I'm Sorry," these words I try to keep tame.

"I'm Sorry," words I mutter from dusk till dawn.
"I'm Sorry," words right before my final yawn.
"I'm Sorry," but I feel crushed all the while.
"I'm Sorry," I say with a smile.

"I'm Sorry," the final words from a broken man.
"I'm Sorry," the words that crush a faithful fan.
"I'm Sorry," I shout with all the air from my lung.
"I'm Sorry," the only words I knew when I was young.

"I'm Sorry," words I say much too often.
"I'm Sorry," words much too easy to soften.
"I'm Sorry," words I'll say at my final stand.
"I'm Sorry," a symphony played by the band.

"I'm Sorry," my final call for help.
"I'm Sorry," no one hears, it's but a yelp.
"I'm Sorry," words I'll cry from the depths of hell.
"I'm Sorry," words I know all too well.

- Ayden V.

Charleston County School of the Arts

I am in the minority.

I am in the minority.
I won't bow to the white man.
I'll shoot this pretty face
Before anyone touches me.

I'm thicker than I look
Blacker than the night
Guns arranging, guns blazing
Forced on the ground.

Have you ever heard of the game called the police says?
Well if you haven't! Join along with me!
It's when you do everything the police say
but if the police don't say to do it don't do it! Get it?!
Ok, follow me along!

Police say put your hands up!
Police say get on the ground!
Don't make another sound!
Why did you make a sound, huh?!
Do what the police tell you to do!
Sorry it's your first time playing, police will take it easy on you.
No! Do it right, no mistakes.
How come you're still making mistakes huh!?
Do what the police tell you!

Police say shoot the black men!
Police shoot the black women!
Police say shoot the black kid!
Police say shoot the Person of color!
Shoot them!

Why didn't you shoot them!?
I said shoot 'em! The police said shoot 'em!
Shoot the white man!
Good you listen.
Never shoot when the police don't tell you too.
Shoot them! Shoot them! Shoot them!
Why aren't you shooting them!?
It wouldn't matter if I didn't say shoot them!
be silent.
Sit still.
Hold your breath.
Await execution.
Police say kill them.

I´m crying my tears
I can't get up
Please help me momma I'm scared
Tell my sister I didn't mean it
I promised daddy I´d succeed
Bubba, please I'm sorry

They got me in cuffs I'm singing
To the lord to take me
Blood has shuddered from my lips
My two-toned precious lips
I'm quivering
I'm shivering
I'm mirroring your face
I'm on the floor im beaten up
And bruises on my waist

My love is so sincere I promise baby I'm here
I swear ill make it another day
I don't wanna die, not yet god, please!
I have a family!
I want a baby!

Let me bless my aunties, my uncles
I wanna see my grandmama and my grandaddy
Before the holy bible
Great horror I face let me see my brothers and sisters
Before the days over
Please don't make me scream
Only when the day through

I'm finna escape like Harriet man.
Underground I'll be on that bus with Rosa.
By your own people's Tyre.
I can't breathe, said George.
Breonna momma crying man you took her baby.
On god, I´m finna see Emmett till
And my wrong boy executed George Stinney.
I´m sorry babies, I know it was
wrong of them.. cops won't rot
But they go in all our hearts.

Bless me with holy matrimony
Let me have my kids
Give me a job
Don't put me underground
Let me speak
Let me yell
Let me see
Let me be
Free...

You know I can't do that
You know what you are
I curse for you to bow down
To sing to the white man
Ignite no flame
But prosper the same
You will be dead in the minority den.

-*Zoe H.*

Goose Creek High School

Gentle note: Some of the poems in this section use adult language and deal with adult themes.

Music has made me

Music has made me,
It's the graphite in the pencil that wrote out my history
It's attached to every memory
So when they read my eulogy they better remember the melody My name means harmony
It's infused with the blood that connects my family It's that sweet symphony that sits on tip of my tongue

My music grounds me

But...
Music ain't just about me,
It's memories mixed with history

Moma smiles when she hears the same Salt-n-Pepa, shoop, and Lola from the coppa dancing down the same hallways she did when she was my age

Daddy laughs knowin' who's in Paris as I blast N.W.A. from my bedroom speakers Ty reminisces the day he taught me how to whip and nae nae
JJ nods his head to the beat
of the lo-fi jazz he so gifted me

Uncle Buggy plays roundabout on his guitar while I'm playing with dolls at my grandma's house Pause

Mama, I found my calling,
I'm an eclectic kid with a love for pop, punk, lo-if, jazz, hip hop, rock Anything I can get my hands on, Becomes a beat in the balled on me
In my story music is that mosaic that created my personality, so mixed up I may be just know I'm incredibly happy

Mama, I'm happy

And I, am a part of this family
A family that has and will continue to infuse our
children with a heartbeat like a metronome and vocal
chords to find new tones
They will find their melody

So when my baby cousins come to me,
Asking what is our legacy, hidden inside our family
history
I'll guide them happily to listen to that sweet
cacography, the sound of everyone
marching to the beat of their own drums
I'll set the sticks in their hands lovingly and watch as
they play their first melody as simple as it may be it's
the first step to see how music will make them, just as
music has made me.

- Arya I.

The demon in me

I close my eyes
I bite my tongue
Breathe in
Breathe out

My mother raises her hands to the heavens
Spits flies out of her holy mouth
And burns my face

"Demon I rebuke you"

My muscles tense
As tears welled up in my eyes

"Demon I rebuke you"

She screams to a god I do not understand
She speaks in tongues that I can't comprehend

I know who I am, I know what I said, I know what I meant,and yet I shake

The space between us is my saving grace
As she cuts the air with her hands

"Why do you flinch?"

"I am your provider, your keeper,
so why do you flinch?"

I taste blood in my mouth, not daring to loosen my tongue "Answer me"

Her hands adjust my chin like putting a ball on a tee

"Look at me"

My stained eyes meet with the fire behind her windows

She quickly tries to put out the fire

"Lord, please. Show me my daughter" I don't move

- Arya I.

{no name}

I can hear my warm breaths in a cold dark abyss of nothingness, there is a sharp pain that runs across my neck, that feels like it's severing me from my own body. I can't feel anything but the pain that drags across it. A pain like sharp pins stabbing over and over, and I can't breathe. Was I ever breathing in the first place? How long have I been like this? I can't move, I can't breathe, I have to get out, I have to, I have to I have to. Wait there's something. A hand I can see it. It's a light in the darkness or maybe an angel's hand trying to save me from the hell of eternal darkness and pain, but I can't move. I feel as if I'm melting into the darkness as the hand is slowly fading from my view. Don't leave me here! Please take me with you! I want to live, I need to live. Suddenly as if that thought alone was the only thing strapping me down. My eyes shot open. I didn't even know they were closed but now I am grateful they're not. I can see my mom and my brother hovering over me on each side, my mother eyes are closed, but my brother is looking down at me. He smiles and hugs me, and soon my mother follows too. My
brother smiled and hug me. Something must have happened he's never done that. I sit up slowly with my mother's help and look around me. I'm in a hospital. I don't know why but I don't care. The pain in my neck has gone and I can see. After a little more time a man in a white coat walks in. At first, he looks grim but when he looks at me his eyes grow wide. He looks at my mother and brother and smiles. It's a miracle. I don't really remember what he said after that.
I think I drifted off to sleep. But as I return to that familiar darkness. Instead of it being a cold, lonely darkness, it's warm, like cuddles by a fire and it's still dark but I'm not strapped down anymore. I'm floating.

- Arya I.

Forever 160

You know life is bad,
when the bile rising up your throat—
into a toilet—
can taste more like home
than your gran's award winning mac & cheese

That's what words do to you,
what numbers whisper to you,
what the scale shows you.

Food is no longer a pleasure but an obligation,
to keep yourself alive.

To soothe your hunger for the perfect body,
the right number,
the good weight.

Food is no longer a memory but a fear.

I don't eat ice cream anymore.
Or fast food,
or pumpkin pie.
Not even the hot cocoa drinks
you find in your mother's arms at midnight.
I wait till the night envelopes my house,
I exercise for hours desperate for perfection,
brushing aside my stomach eating itself alive—
I'm only alive to hear my mother say "you're pretty, sweetie!"

Cara said "Beauty is pain"
and I think pain is worth the wait.

The scales never went up.
The scales never went down.

160.
161.
160.
165.
159.
160.

The number 160 is more unlucky to me than 13,
what would it be like to be 130?
I'll never know.

The scales do me injustice,
and no balancing of diets
or late night crunches
can take away the feeling,
of not feeling pretty.

- *bri m.*

Could Never Please Myself

People come and go,
but suppression stays forever.
I was taught to use my voice,
but only when others wished to hear it.
Never speak too loud,
never laugh too hard,
listen to authority and respect will be yours.
I was never allowed to question,
not as a child, not as teen,
because you can't control a puppet
if they make their own strings.

I was conditioned to please,
ask the ocean of people in my life,
"Are you okay? Don't you worry about me."
Obedience was beaten into me,
bruises lines my mind to this day—
I weep every morning—
wondering where
that girl went with her loving little heart.

Wondering how the world could be this dark,
wondering how suppression can
take away any expression this little girl ever had,
wondering if I'll ever take my strings back
and play with my own thoughts,
and I wonder two hard questions,
Can a people pleaser ever
please themselves enough?
Has conditioning and following corrupted me
so, so much,
that I will never think I'm enough?

- *bri m.*

trial and error

you were a "trial subscription"
and I liked what I saw,
presented yourself as
sweet movies of love
a guy with a heart,
gentleman characteristics and
I've never been a love interest,
but I pressed start.

you said you were a trial,
7 days for me to see,
to test out,
to explore,
but you sucked me into one of your delusions
and added my name to your watchlist of sorts.

I couldn't break out,
the glass of the tv too strong,
and your arms were around me in the rain,
I heard the watchers "awww"
I pounded my fists against you,
this wasn't what I wanted,
the rain was turning black,
had me feeling I was being haunted

I didn't want you anymore.

I didn't realize how charming you were,
you're like the main character
who can't recognize they can hurt
let me go,
I only asked for 7 days,

let me go,
please,
I'm asking nicely, I'm asking politely,
I've been your perfect love interest and treated you right,
unwrap your arms around mine,
don't hold me tight,

and let me free.

your arms burn,
I only have my words
for an extinguisher,
but you don't have the want to listen.
you're flaming,
i plead,
holes enclose into my chest and i lose my breath

I feel unsafe,
I want to cancel my subscription to your name.
I don't want this show,
I don't want to be the love interest anymore,
please,
let me go,
my trial ended so long ago,
this button isn't working,
"Error, please try again!"

just listen to me for once,
if you loved me,
you'd let me go.

- bri m.

Listen to yourself

Hey Momma?
What boy?
Actually nevermind, listen to yourself
I can hear pretty clearly.
As clear as my stomach grumbling
Boy, stop.

As clear as the crystalline tears running away from my
bright eyes
Stop crying before I give you something to cry about.
But Momma, I'm hungry!
But nothing.

Am I nothing? And I know you ain't bluffing.
Because this face doesn't remember a moment where
you hesitated
Hesistated to hit
Hesistated to care about no one but
Yourself
C'mon now listen to yourself
Yourself is all you speak about
Go ahead, keep on dissing me now
I can't help but kiss my purple bruises
NOW MOMMA

Watch your tone when you talk to me boy.

Now I've watched my tone for long enough.
How about we trade spots, take what I got.
NOW MOMMA
How about you watch your tone
Listen to yourself before you speak

Why you crying?
I'll give you something to cry about.
About someone who had a kid but the kid don't want her.
About how you try to be so involved now...
Even when you were there
Your hands were more involved than your feelings.
Now your eyes hissing at me, fix yo damn face!
Me? Ungrateful?
Maybe, but when you can't
Give me the bare minimum
You can't be human
DON'T ASK FOR NOTHING
NOW MOMMA

Who's ungrateful now?
I choose to come to your house
I choose to slave away with a broom and a mop
Back then I didn't have a choice but you did
Yeah, you didn't give enough care to watch me suffer
You let it happen
You bet on it
And I bet when you lose track of my foot steps you'll be screaming for me

So now I'm scheming about
How imma show you gentle parenting,
How my words will contort better than yours,
My tongue fights more than my fists,
You say I'm just like my father
But you're the one who molded me into him,
Into a father, into the parent
Neither of you could be,
But I won't continue on about him
Because one can change and he's

Stared into mirrors for too long...

My fists raise a little higher
Just like when you beat him
Just like you raised me
Just like you needed a duplicate
JUST WHO DID MORE DAMAGE THAN I COULD
MANAGE WITHOUT CHANGE

Yeah I damaged your body, coming into this world
But I was just getting ready
For the war you were starting.
NOW MOMMA
LOOK AT ME WHEN I TALK TO YOU
I have a reason to cry
Do you?!

Look at the strain in my eyes when you realize
I am the one who raised your kids, my siblings,
My brother, more like me than
Anyone he lays his eyes on.
Look at the pain permeating my pupils.
The ones you blackened, the medicated rags
That covered my face, like some white flag
That I will NEVER surrender to you.

- Caleb S.

A Mother's Attempt at Love

I love you is something every child should hear their mom say
Say it with every spare second you have
Because you don't know when it'll turn to never

I never loved you or I never got to say it
It is something I have heard from my mother
But her words have fine print
A contract of lies and abuse

It all escapes her mouth in one sentence
As her lips move flies swarm out buzzing around my ears until I do not know what paper I signed

But what I do know is that if I don't know her every need and want
I will be sued
A contract broken
A payment of punchlines
and thoughts of the 911 hotline

Something I will always be prepared for
Unlike that little boy who was throwing up and crying
The thing that he did not know
Is you did nothing wrong
I did nothing wrong
We did nothing wrong

What is wrong is a mom
that could lie but never love a kid
You get older and start realizing what truth is
Me and my brother started bonding at his age of 8
Him realizing that maybe our sisters can be annoying

But was not up for debate was how mom never wanted to give the time to take care of the kids she wanted so bad to birth
He said brother we always have to ask you for things if we ask mom we end up speaking to you, but sometimes you aren't home and she says mean things

I respond I'm sorry you'll get used to it one day if not look forward into the horizon the sunset all so far
And realize that it is something you may never reach trauma pushing that sunset so far back it becomes a star in a system of dreams
Our shackles will rust one day

I try to keep my siblings happy keep their sun's from becoming stars but as I walk up these steps
with a black eye
It shatters their glass persona that our brother is amazing and strong
He loves us

The only thing that remains in the shards below their feet is
My words of love
Not our moms
And when they look up they will see me dragging their stars back within arms reach of their tiny hands

Because we knew mom never loved us
Or maybe she did mean it at one point in time
But I can never decipher the difference between her lies and truth anymore
I do not want her love
And nor will I ever give it to her

- Caleb S.

Pills Drive Zombies

Hey, have you ever noticed
that adults love to call teenagers Zombies?
They label us as dead, decaying,
but sometimes able to move
They call us non communicating
groaning and emotionless beings

But the thing they should really be talking about is...

Zoloft is a virus adults feed to stitch their children's zombie mouths shut.
We teens grasp the pills with outstretched hands in an attempt to replace the serotonin we don't have the privilege to get at home
Though our hands weaken and we drop the pills our bodies drop we can't stop being zombies for adults as our brains pop
Prozac force-fed to us like hard to swallow flesh
In an attempt to cover the pain, the strain on our bodies never dissipate
We're asking ourselves to shut out the world as our eyes shut out life...
I'd like to think adults care but they shove bottles of Celexa down our throats before they ask to hear our silenced words, the pain worsened by the thought of happiness

They blame our zombifying pills on us,
but truly, we'd like to flip the blame
The blame of stress, the blame of not being able to press on, the blame of not being able to stay awake
to pass the test
This test of life

But we can only blame them in silence
for fear of choking on the bottles
of Lexapro lodged in our throats
Before we could croak the vocal cords broke
The mindless strokes pain us as we're classified as fake

1 in 6 U.S. youth aged 6-17 experience
a mental health disorder each year
50% of all lifetime mental illnesses begin by age 14
Suicide is the 2nd leading cause of death among people
aged 10-34
And you have the audacity to call us zombies?
When you're able to address everything you need or
want
Yet your kids drag themselves around with nothing but
pain in their darkened eyes,
Do we blame you oh wait we can't because it's our fault
We don't have anything to stress about we're young
How about you tell that to the kids
who were pushed to the edge
You should be responsible for the problems you create
As you say you are responsible for us

The Zoloft, Prozac, Celexa, Lexapro you feed,
we swallow as we read the labels:
"Take 1 tablet by mouth every day"
it's the only compassion we get
We'd like to be given the antidote
not just pre-installments
Antidotes to your ignorance, antidotes you deny us
that contains the love and support and understanding
we want, no,
that we deserve

Or soon,
all your eyes will see and all your ears
will hear is nothing but the pain of our silence
when others watch as you read:
"Take 1 tablet by mouth every day."

when you dismiss these walking zombies
in front of you,
and watch them turn into ghosts...

- Caleb S.

BROKEN

I am broken.
I've been hurt, bruised,
and scared by people i thought i could trust.
It's like every single day my heart is being crushed.
And yes i'm tired, and yes i'm in pain,
But the blood from the scars
you caused are still stained.
At least in my heart,
You left me all alone when i was sinking in the dark.
You left me when i felt as if i was falling apart.
Please don't try and help, acting like you care now.
The pain and suffering is something i don't fear now.
I can't find happiness, only peace.
I haven't found neither,
i'm happy on the outside, inside i'm deceased.
I don't want to be me,
i don't want to be the person i am.
But sooner or later i will have to relive this pain again.

- Le'Mar S.

OLD ME

If i'm being honest, i miss the old me.
The old me that was full of joy and so happy.
Or the me that didnt feel like
he wasn't really important or castaway.
The new me version on me is just dead inside.
All my feelings i had to learn how to set aside.
The new version has a hard time trusting.
The new me just wants to love,
but has a hard time loving.
My head is hurting, reminiscing about the past.
I swear i was the old me just yesterday.
But my mom said that i'm growing up just a lil too fast.
Now i have to accept the fact that i will never be the same.
Now I have to keep growing up,
suffering with the same pain.

- *Le'Mar S.*

ME vs ME

In this world, it's always been me vs me.
Cause for some reason, i always felt alone.
There's only one way i can fix that,
And that's by reading this poem.
There was always a point in my life where i thought the world was letting me down,
Till i realized it was me,
i was the one letting myself down.
Everyday i would have conversations with myself. I've been trying to figure who i am since i was twelve.
I try and tell myself, please, Le'mar, please, don't stress, but my other half proves, once again, that he's the best.

- *Le'Mar S.*

The Woman in the Mirror

The woman in the mirror
She speaks to me, gently, caressing my body and
whispering in my ear, reaching her hand through the
silver barrier
She tells me that she was born with a curse, that she
was born **hungry**

That she was spat from her mother's womb with this
aching, gnawing feeling in her chest
Surrounding and swallowing its heart, whole,
like a shattering disease, leaving her ravenous
Infecting her body and life with the act of wanting, a
need for something that she could never obtain,
something she could never reach

So every night, when she reaches through my mirror,
standing over me, her skin wilting over her bones like a
layer of thin paint - she feeds on me.

Every night, when her hunger comes, and her false body
is too empty for her to handle, She feeds on me.

When she speaks to me, it is in a low voice, her words
come out in between shallow breaths, and they slip out
from between her crackling lips—

She tells me secrets sometimes, shameful stories filled
with obscure details and remnants of what
her life once was.

She says that her mother's hunger came in the evening,
right before the sunset.

And as that sun disappeared last night, the woman's last shred of safety became fleeting with the light of the day–

She could hear the screaming. It slipped out and wavered over her, laying down thickly like a blanket of fog

While her mother's aching enveloped her completely, gnawing at every last piece of her like a wild animal. Letting her own hunger eat away at her until it engulfed her being completely, shrouding any last string of love left inside her.

She never fed on the woman, leaving her body to rot and spoil, bloating into something unrecognizable, her heart swelling as the bacteria circled it within her chest.

The animal comes to me at night
She crawls towards me, on all fours

Maggots creep up from her rotting ankles, consuming what little is left of her murky flesh as her nails scritch and scratch at the tiled floor

She comes to my torso, sinking her greasy fingers into my stomach, while I lay powerlessly, pulling away at my layers of skin as she begins to chew and chew and chew

Considering my innards, my intestine slips through her gaping mouth and down her slick throat.
Biting on my fat like the gristle on a steak, like a wolf devouring their prey when my veins are caught, hung, lazily from the gaps in her yellowed teeth

Bits and pieces of my sliced body dance around in her stomach, and my own skin dangles from the ends of her claws as blood spurts out like fountains from my open wounds

She relishes in the overwhelming feeling of my blood, my essence, dripping down her front It snakes down the cracks in her skin, forming a pool of warm, foul, liquid at her feet

She fuels herself, like a vehicle with gasoline, stuffing herself to her core with the energy my body once possessed until it spilled out from every orifice on her My blood clots and curdles when it pours from the tear in my heart, and she rips at it like a dog with their favorite chew toy, a nibble here and there while I sink deeper into my bathroom floor.

But when the woman is no longer hungry, and she finally appears to be satisfied, my dried blood still remaining in the crevices between her teeth -

She stitched me up carefully, closing up my exposed body with her needle and the thread of her kind words When I lay there, an empty husk of myself, my body all stitched and raw My stomach sitting emptily, my thoughts echoing in the bareness of it And it begins to ache when I feel my own, familiar hunger,

I look in the mirror to recognize the woman staring back at me, my own body torn and sewed into itself - my disconnected tongue slipping out from between my oily lips... reaching for something to satisfy me

- Conner P.

Untitled

'Sigh', here we go.
Life, the unforgiving, complete pain in the ass... let's talk about it!
It's great, isn't it? Yeah, I'm trying to make this as positively sarcastic as possible.
Life sucks, it's horrible, unforgiving, and a complete ass that does whatever it wants.
Life does not care whether you're 1, 35, 63, or the healthiest person alive.
Life will screw you over with the worst possible things.
I, for one, know this to be true because of my dad.
He was a very good man and quite healthy.
He had a good life,
and life, being the slimy, undercooked dishwasher pineapple it is,
saw how good he was doing and said, "Hey, you know what, since you're doing so good, how about I give you a life-threatening disease that will most definitely kill you in the near future?"
And that's exactly what it did.
It gave him the worst possible disease that really did kill him only like a few months after his diagnosis.
And I mean, we've all had at least one "I'm doing great and then – boom – your mom has an incurable cancer, is now blind, and has frickin' heart disease" life situation.
Now that's just an example, but if this genuinely has happened to someone, I just want to say I am very sorry and I hope your life gets better in the future.
But seriously, screw life.
And with that being said,

may life's bed be filled with cracker crumbs,
Legos in its shoes,
and may you all have a blessed rest of your day.

- Olivia R.

Untitled

I miss the old days.
The old days when you weren't judged for not having the latest iPhone 99 pro x max.
The days when us kids could just be kids and not worry about getting kidnapped on our own front lawn.
The days when you could wear what you wanted to without getting hateful stares.
The days where you could say whatever you wanted to without being called a slur just because of how you speak.
When you could go outside without being body-shamed for eating a chicken nugget from McDonald's.
The days when you could walk to school with almost no fear of being kidnapped by some pervert in a white van.
God, I miss the old days,
And I wish they could come back.
But life doesn't work that way,
And now we're left with the memories of the days when kids could go outside in the yard and play until they hear their mother call, "Kids, come in! It's dinner time!"
I miss the old days,
But they can't come back.
They're gone and over with,
And the only thing I can do now is dream about going back to the old days and being able to live life to the true fullest without fear and judgment.

- Olivia R.

Untitled

Mother, please, I need you to understand.
I really have been trying my best.
I know my grades aren't the best right now.
It's impossible to focus, and I can't think straight half the time.
But at least I try.
I try to have better grades.
I'm trying to be a better daughter.
But no matter how hard I try, I just can't get it right.
No matter how hard I try to fix things between us,
I always screw it up and make things worse.
I've been trying and trying, but nothing ever works.
I have no idea how to make you see that I'm trying,
And the only thing I can do is keep lying,
Say everything is fine and move on with my day,
Hoping and praying that no one finds out,
Hiding my problems, making sure no one sees
Just how messed up my mind is, constantly degrading me,
Making me believe that everyone hates me.
And the only thing I can do is write this out,
Not knowing how to tell anyone what I'm feeling.
The only thing I wish is for you to understand,
And I hate every time you put that on me,
Expecting me to deal with it and not complain.
And the only thing that I can really say is I'm sorry.
I'm sorry for not meeting your expectations.
I'm sorry that I don't know how to show that I love you.
I'm sorry that I'm such a screw up,
And I'm sorry that I don't know how to be a good daughter.
So I'm throwing my emotions into this poem,

Writing and writing to try and heal my own soul,
Listening to this and finding out it's all true,
And I just want you to know that I really do love you.

- *Olivia R.*

Worlds Without End (1)

in another life, you are writing a suicide note in a sun-lit
room. so barren, so parched –

this is what you define as *"perfect moment"*
because the hollowness of this hour, leaves a moment
for you to cry.

you hated sentimentality
when it was seen.

all the words and red rainfall spill,
bleeding onto the page

if only we could turn and read what it stained, but
understanding can only go so far –

out of the gun's chamber,
  some sullen air of apathy
infiltrating the night,

you were always impatient.

worlds with no end, you begin the memorial.

        in this letter I imagine you write about the way
        you held your sister's hand
        in the mid-August heat,
        wandering some city block of north charleston

          crows pecking at the
          bullets,
              the beer bottles,
              and deflated footballs –

you describe letting go of her hand,
        running a few centimeters away, to risk a
        glimpse of freedom you let
        the smoke beam onto your face.

you are home and this is everything.

I never told anyone at your funeral what you might've written.

I didn't want to be wrong.

I dug my shoes in the dirt. I know what you felt.

damn shame, I thought.

- Erik H.

an ode to a trip

we drift off,
        like worried rain,   into ourselves,

we call into the stillness,
        swallowed by this house, the grass
        breathing the scraps off our hearts,

        we can't hear anything,
the sound of your name becomes
mine,
    we bleed red, after all.

    you tell me, this is how god
    works,
        that
    we are carrying a prepared separation
truths are known, lies are created

i say, sure,
    but all i really know is that i'll miss this

we swallow one more pill, and we soar farther
    sunk below, body frozen,

all the noises, blended into spring, all these scars made
into roses — nothing remains of my skin,
and yet i still want to bleed, abuse, and repeat

        fused green,
      solitary souls,
        an impenetrable and
        warm.
        silence
            and then the police are here.

I never saw you again, after that.
You were gone into memory.

I meant to tell you, what I dreamt of, while I laid,
vomit-stained, underneath the shadow of a sharp blue
angel. I dreamt we were children, chasing each other
down a mountain. We found some sort of love in that.

Burning memories are harder than flushing pills.
Sleepless nights, a vague nostalgia sweeping my tongue.
I'm walking away from the graves we've dug.

But one day, when we are proper cogs in the machine,
and we clock out of some dirty office, I hope you will
remember that we existed.

I hope you too, will lay down to sleep, and dream it all
one more time as if we were back at 17 again,

carving a forbidden utopia —

and that'll be the end of it. carry on.

- Erik H.

Sounds

Sounds.

What are sounds?

Vibrations that travel through air,

And can be heard when they reach a person's ear.

Sounds.

The only thing to reach my ear was you.
You and that perfect voice of yours,
That perfect imitation of nails on a chalkboard,
That came from your mouth.
That was the only sound I heard.

To this day,
That is the only sound I hear.
To this day,
Two years later,
I can still hear your voice.

Why can I still hear your voice?
Is this what you wanted?
Did you dream of your voice
clinging to the back of my mind,
Like the plague?
Did you dream,
That I would never forget you?

I guess I should congratulate you,

You got your wish after all.

Congratulations,
I cannot walk in a crowded room.

Congratulations,
I cannot walk when someone is behind me.

Congratulations,
I cannot walk,
when my friends are not in my line of sight.

Why is it,
That we only hear what we do not wish to hear?
Your voice plays through my head,
Like a song I cannot forget.
But boy,
Do I regret listening to this song.

Do you consider yourself a bully?
What even is a bully?
If I had to define it,
Your name would be the first to come to my mind.

Your large hair,
Must have been made to keep all of your evil plans,
Locked away.

Does anyone even know what you did?
I wonder,
Did you enjoy it?
Do you reminisce with all of your friends,
Around a large, inviting fire,
While you are all roasting marshmallows in my misery?

Do you even remember me?
Or was I just a fun pastime for you?
Well,
I certainly remember you.
I remember you,
And the loud scream,
That pierced my eardrums,
When you were around.

Was it fun to sneak up on me?
Was I an easy victim?
Was it fun to scream in my ear?

Why did you do it?
Was it just some jokes shared between friends?
Was that it?
Did you think we were friends?

It's been two years now,
And life is still a struggle.
Do you even know the pain you caused me?
I thought it would end,
That everything would go back to normal after you had stopped.
But it has been two years,
Two years,
And I still flinch.

When there is chatter happening behind me,
When I am in a loud area,
When someone is just walking behind me, I flinch.
When someone sneaks up on me,
When a door opens,

When someone speaks out of the blue, I flinch.

You caused this,
And you should be held accountable.
I find it heinous,
That you can do this to a person.
It is heinous that you can change
How a person functions,
And not even care.
You did not even shed a tear.

- Alexandria G.

I Have a Dream

Dreams,
A series of thoughts, images,
And sensations occurring
in a person's mind during sleep.

I have a dream,
A dream that has followed me
Through my sleep,
Since I was a young child,
Far younger than I am now.

A young child,
Already exposed to the truth of the world.

A young child,
Whose mind was filled with atrocities.
A young child,
Whose mind already knew the phrase,
"Not everything in the world is fair."

I have a dream,
A dream where children are not told,
"You need to be mature now,"
"You are too old for that."

A dream where a child is a child,
Until they are ready for what the world will throw at them.

A dream where innocence will cloud their mind,
Until they are ready for evil to coincide
with that innocence.

I have a dream. In this dream,
Children remain innocent,
Blind to the truth of the world.

The youth are happy,
And the youth are free to enjoy
Whatever their creative minds
find them wishing to enjoy.

In this dream,
They do not have to wish to enjoy something.

In this dream,
Teachers do not take away their creativity,
Adults do not taint their imagination,
Older children do not steal their innocence.

Because in this dream,
Children are free to be children,
And do as a child should do,
Be a child.

Dreams,
I have a dream.

In this dream,
Children are allowed to dream.
The youth are allowed to do as the youth do,
And dream of whatever their beautiful minds can conjure.

I have a dream,
A dream where your child,
Can dream of becoming a princess, a king,
A teacher,

The president,
Can dream of whatever real,
Or fantastical thing,
They wish to dream of.

I have a dream,
Where your children,
And future children,
Are free to be children.
Free as they are intended to be.

I have a dream,
A dream where teachers do not
Wish maturity upon a child,
That is at heart,
Still a child.

I have a dream,
A beautiful dream where adults do not,
Vandalize the dream of a child.

I have a dream,
That one day,
Children will not have to stop being children.
Where the point a child stops being a child,
Does not come until they are no longer a child.

I have a dream,
That one day,
Children will not stop being children,
While they are still young,
And deep down,
Still children.
Children hoping to dream,
Children dreaming of having a dream.

Dreams,
A series of thoughts, images,
And sensations occurring
in a person's mind during sleep.

I have a dream,
Where this is not a dream.
A dream of a time,
Of a place,
Where this does not just accompany my sleep.

I have a dream,
Where this is not a dream.
A dream of a time,
Where this is more than a dream.

In my dream,
This is the reality.

In my dream,
Others have taken the step,
To make this more than a dream.

In my dream,
People realize that what they are doing is hurting us.

I have a dream,
That the children are left
to be children.
Let the children dream.

- Alexandria G.

Dandelions

Dandelions,
Innocent flowers, that just *are,*

Sucking in, all the *bad* in the air,
Little white balls of fluff,
swaying *side* by *side*, in a field of *green*,
Waiting for the day,
when their thin, feathers blow with the wind.

Adults, should be like dandelions,
They, are *not*.
Dandelions forgive,

They exist throughout their short,
seemingly meaningless, lives
Unaware, of the *strain* humans carry.

They float around,

Weightless,

Unburdened,
by the standards set around them.

Adults, should be like *dandelions*,
But, *they* are *not*.
Adults are cruel *beings*,
with *too much time*
to stow in their *grudges*,
and *ideals*.

They *fight*,
through their long lives,
A never ending *journey*,
that drags *on* and *on*,

Their anger is their *friend*,
Accompanying them throughout their journey,
like a bag of *rocks*,
Weighing them *down*,
until it is the only *familiar* thing,
in their lives.

Humans, hold onto everything,
Like a baby, clinging to their mothers warmth,
They latch on to anything,
that crosses their path,
Warm or not,
Real or not.

Humans and dandelions will never be the same,
But, maybe,
If they were,
Even if for just a minute,
We could be free of our burdens,
Free like the dandelions that float around in the clear sky,
Free like the dandelions that lay in fields,
Surrounded by other dandelions,
Free to just be.

Babies are like dandelions,
The only form of human to truly be free of all burden,
Unaware of the emotions surrounding them.
Humans are not like babies.
Humans do not latch onto warmth;

They latch onto the thought of warmth.

Dandelions hold on to the warm caress of the sun's hand,
Their feather-like pappus hold on to the warm promises of a child,
As they're carried through the warm air.
Humans are not like dandelions.
Humans cling to what they perceive as warmth,
Even when that warmth is a broken promise or a cold slap to the face.
Humans latch on to the idea of things.

Humans latch on to idols.
They latch on to the idea of an amazing person that will care about them and can do no wrong.
They latch on to the idea of what this person would look like with short hair, bright clothes, and jewelry, and tan skin.
They latch on to the idea of what this person would look like with long hair, dark clothes, less jewelry, and pale skin.
They hold on to this idea of the perfect person,
Whether or not this idol is that person.
Nobody is perfect.
I guess it's a good thing idols aren't human.

They are a doll for others to play dress-up with,
An emotionless Barbie from your toddler's dreams,
An idea for people to love one day and hate the next.
People do not care about an idol;
They care about the lead role of their fantasy
And the image they must uphold,
The only image the cameras are allowed to see.
Humans care about the image their minds conjure

through dreams and insecurities,
Because who cares if that image is reality?
They are not human, anyway.

Humans are not like dandelions.
Dandelions are innocence personified,
Heaven's flower,
Small clouds that came to befriend the earth.
Dandelions are pieces of the sun that came down to warm the grass.
Humans are not like dandelions.

- Alexandria G.

Untitled

I find it near impossible to hate anyone,
But *you* are a special exception.
Although we weren't always this way.

Before it all came crashing down,
We were all each other had.
Sword and shield in our hands,
Ready to take on whatever the world threw at us.

But now,
I would rather extend endless mercies to strangers
Before even *thinking* of giving you the time of day.
And I can't figure out why.

Because in reality,
All you have ever needed from me was my sympathy.
At heart, you are only a little boy
Who's been battered and broken
beyond either of our understanding.

Yet you still dream of changing the world
With your stories that form
From your bottomless pools of creativity
That leak from your brain
And drip onto the page,
Carefully and patiently crafting each and every character,
Every scene unlike the last.

But you are also your worst enemy.
You meticulously orchestrate songs of lies

Made from melodic music of disdain and deceit
I and others so callously provided.
And I beg you,
Don't listen to them.
Don't listen to me.

Yes, you may have flaws.
You are not perfect.
But I'll be damned
If you think that is all you are.

You are worth so much more than you know.
Listen to those who love you.
Listen to how they say
Your love is enough.
Your presence is enough.
You are enough.

I just want to give you the world you so desperately try to give others.
But all I ever manage to do
Is give you all of my hatred.
And for that, I'm so sorry.
Because all you have ever deserved was my love.

- Jose O.

Untitled

"You're a good kid, you know that?"
No, I don't.
Because every time
I hear those 7 little words,
The same question
rings in my head for countless hours:
"Am I really?"

Am I really this good person I'm made out to be?
Because I don't really feel like I am,
Not anymore.
I know at some point I was,
But honestly it was so long ago,
Should it even count?
'Cause I'm no good kid now.

Grab a thesaurus and you'll see,
My name is just another synonym for failure.
I'm an 8-letter word scramble that spells out disaster,
And by the time you decipher me, it's far too late for you,
Because everywhere I go, destruction follows.
I've let my closest friendships and bonds succumb
To a creature I swore to never let myself become.
So tell me, what good kid am I?!

And here I am begging and pleading
to be free from this hell I've created.
Knowing all too well I'll never accept the help I need,
Because I've descended so far into my own madness,
I'm afraid the hands reaching out to save me will just

push me down further.
So I lay trapped
in a burning labyrinth of my thoughts,
Unable to find a way to escape,
Even when the exit door is right in front of my face.

- Jose O.

Laing Middle School

Inside Me

I'm so good at being good
That's the me everybody gets
I don't cheat and I don't cuss
I like school and read books
I'll never drink or do drugs

Sometimes I forget
There's more to me
Than what I should be
There's more of me
Than I let myself be

I'm the girl with a bad mom
I'm the girl who pushes through it
I'm the girl who doesn't need pity
Because she's good

I'm the good girl
But there's a part of me that
No one ever sees
There's a part of me that
I don't let free

She's manipulative and a bit pretentious
She's selfish and cruel
She's angry at her sad mom
She's not so good at all

But she's trying so hard to be kind
She's trying to be honest
But she has to fight the darkness
She trips along the way
But I hope I'll get there someday.

- *June G.*

Moultrie Middle School

My Wishes Of Vain

I look upon
The bright blue sky
And think, how could a day so beautiful
Ever be as sad as this?

I wish I may,
I wish I might,
I wish upon this star tonight.
I wish for a joyful life,
A life of sunshine,
A life of glory,
Definitely not one this gory.

I wish I may,
I wish I might,
I wish my tears away in delight.
For my dreams
Have been achieved
As I am whisked away by your sorrowful speech.

-Isla P.

My Cute Kitten

I love my cats,
They look like bats.
Puss and Boots are their names;
They are as beautiful as majestic flames.

Puss is a kitten,
She looks like a fluffy mitten.
All night long,
Puss sings songs.

Boots is as smart as Einstein,
She is my genuine Valentine.
I love her very much,
Because she makes me blush.

-*William C.*

The Cat

The trees smiled down at the cat,
quietly purring, which was as quiet as a mouse.
His whiskers were a soft pillow.
He woke up and shook off the majestic,
ravishingly red, beautiful butterfly.
He climbed a tree and saw a bird,
which he pounced on and caught that wordy bird that
chirped nonstop, extremely loudly.
Then there was no more noise; it was still.
He was still hungry, so he went by the ocean and caught
some jumbo shrimp.

-William C.

Dreams of Playing Football

I am a football player and like to play football.
I wonder about the world.
I hear people cheer.
I see people cheer.
I want to be a football player.
I am a football player and like to play football.

I pretend to be in the NFL.
I feel the pressure.
I touch the football.
I worry about getting hurt.
I cry when I get hurt, but always get up.
I am a football player and like to play football.

I understand it is hard to get into the NFL.
I say I am going to the NFL.
I dream of going to the NFL.
I push myself.
I hope to become a football player.
I am a football player and like to play football.

- Eli O.

I Am a Boy And a Man

I am a boy and a man.
I wonder what control feels like.
I hear playful noises.
I want money, I want greed.
I am a boy and a man.

I pretend to act older than I am.
I feel not as powerful as I would like.
I touch on sensitive feelings.
I worry about my future, my success.
I cry when I am alone, but I try not to.
I am a boy and a man.

I understand what I am meant to know.
I say and act out regretful things.
I dream of a bigger, more broad life.
I try my best to be a "good human."
I believe that I am at my best.
I am a boy and a man.

- *T.B*

Nature's Touch

I flutter my wings,
For what nature brings.
I feel the bond,
In which I am fond.

The feline opens up to life,
Free of struggle and eternal strife.
It relaxes as I passively land,
On which it counts to hold its breath.

In between my eternal stare,
It glances a majestic glare.
An abstract bond of fur to wing,
Like the push and pull of water.

In the likeness of mortal life,
The eternal love of wildlife,
I feel the bond which nature brings,
And the song in which it sings.

- Evan W.

I am Human

I beg to look like others,
To feel pretty, to be liked,
To be enjoyed.
I forget I am human and have feelings.

They push me down, and I let them.
Suddenly I can't get back up.
I am stuck in this hole of anxiety and self-hate.
Then I see the light.

It reaches out to me, and I can breathe.
I am treated like a person, a human being.
I am a person, I have feelings.
I am human.

- Anonymous

A Drowning Memory

I aim for the peaks but my valleys are low,
I can never determine who they are, friend or foe.
The damages needed to mend and so I did sow,
Whether rain or fire, sleet or snow.

These years are when ambition begins to grow,
The fear that drowns us or the winds that blow.
They said that only time would ever know
The soft sound of simple song,
That everybody would sing along,
Although a place no one would go,
A place where a dried river used to flow.

As the sun fades to night,
I fear, and I have great fright,
As I am pushed away from the place,
I fear I leave without a trace.

- Caroline L.

Echoes

I'm hurt and loved, it's true, you see,
I wonder, do they care for me?
I hear whispers, sneaky, sly.
I see my friends, right by my side.
I want them close, no distance to be,
I'm hurt and loved, in harmony.

I act like I don't hear a sound,
But their words hit hard, all around.
I touch my friend, so near, so dear,
Yet I fear they'll leave, my heart's unclear.
I cry when they rescue, set me free,
I'm hurt and loved, it's plain to see.

I grasp the words they chose to speak,
But in response, I stay meek.
I dream of shouting, strong and tall,
But I try to hide, not show at all.
I hope someday, I'll rise above,
All I know is, I'm hurt and loved.

- Grayson C.

Untitled

The young girl,
Gladly gracing at the beach.
Many people will teach
The young, graceful girl.

The orange balloon
Rises up in the air.
The sky takes it in his care.
The sky gets many visitors,
But the sky is just an observer
To the young, graceful girl
Gladly gracing at the beach.

- Lucas S.

Respectful of All

I am kind to all and respectful of the natural world.
I wonder if global warming will end.
I hear the beautiful birds
bouncing from tree to tree, chirping.
I see a bright future for everyone here—
a future for Earth, a future for us.
I want to see the people take action
against climate change.
I am kind to all and respectful of the natural world.

I pretend to be kind to others, even if I don't like them.
I feel joy to life and happiness for everyone.
I touch the emotions of anger and sadness.
I worry if kindness can end in violence.
I cry for all the dead, sick, and poor.
I am kind to others and respectful of the natural world.

I understand that history will repeat itself, and if people
don't want to change,
I say we need to make sure that it doesn't happen.
I dream that the oceans
and forests will thrive once again.
I try to help other kids.
I hope that the world
can change for the better of all of us.
I am kind to all and respectful of the natural world.

- Ailey E.

The Poet's Gaze

The poet's garden
Only but a piece of the passions of hers
At her retreat, our capacity is deterred
Even the sly snake can be pardoned

The poet's bench
By ireful clouds, commonly drenched
Here, she can rest
For she remains patient in her scene stripped of stress

The poet's gaze
At a time unknown, strewn to me
To her heart, the right perception is key
Her known adoration will leave none astray

—poem by Scarlett Baker

Intertwined

The cat and the butterfly
The cat is cast as a villain
claws sharp, always hunting
yet the butterfly is a poison to birds

Our beauty is the butterfly
Complex patterns, always praised
Not once has the butterfly been alone
'So why do they impersonate one another?'

The cat wishes for the butterfly's life
It wishes for once, to be the beauty
To never have people turn their backs
But instead praise them, nothing predetermined

The butterfly wishes for the cat's life
a fixed timeline, low expectations
To truly connect with another
Unable to be seen only by colorful patterns

The cat has seen the butterfly's cyclical nature
It sees the pressure, the demand, the expectations
This life, the cat thought to be buoyant and welcoming
The butterfly has a sound yearning for solitude

Their needs can be both implicit and sincere
A breath of fresh air, a break for the years
They're the same, intertwined
The cat and the butterfly

—poem by Scarlett Baker

Ice Skating

The cold air overtakes you as soon as you walk in the door. You sit down on the chairs sitting on the floor. You un zip the bag and take out the shoe. Unthe the laces, they're brand new. You begin to walk over to the ice, & soon as the blade hits you know it'll be nice. The feeling as you glide calmly on the floor, you will never want to walk back to the door.

Scarlett Martin

Porter-Gaud School

I am a performer ...

I am a performer.
I get onstage and I am outspoken and brave
Nerves don't get to me.
I act all nonchalant
Like I have control
But that's not my reality.
I am a performer.
I've learned to hide my crippling anxiety
Behind smiles and false confidence,
Hoping I don't split at the seams.
I am a performer.
I don't know everything.
The control I have is a fallacy,
But I know that everyone else is scared and struggling,
So I bear the burden.
The burden of performing, so there is a steady hand
When you are lost at sea
In the waves and storms of reality.
I am a performer
It gives meaning to a life with no clarity.

- Mika S.

www.ingramcontent.com/pod-product-compliance
Lightning Source LLC
Chambersburg PA
CBHW071238090426
42736CB00014B/3131